50 Herbal Infusions and Tea Recipes

By: Kelly Johnson

Table of Contents

- Chamomile & Lavender Dream
- Peppermint & Lemon Balm Refresh
- Ginger & Turmeric Zing
- Hibiscus & Rose Hip Bliss
- Lemon Verbena & Mint Cooler
- Sage & Honey Elixir
- Rooibos & Vanilla Comfort
- Elderflower & Lime Delight
- Nettle & Dandelion Detox
- Cinnamon & Apple Spice
- Thyme & Lemon Throat Soother
- Lemon Ginger & Cayenne Kick
- Holy Basil & Clove Calm
- Raspberry Leaf & Hibiscus Harmony
- Fennel & Anise Digestive Brew
- Echinacea & Ginger Immune Booster
- Licorice Root & Chamomile Serenity
- Tulsi & Mint Refreshment
- Orange Peel & Cardamom Cheer
- Lavender & Lemonade Fusion
- Marshmallow Root & Peppermint Relief
- Yarrow & Ginger Immunity Boost
- Chai Spiced Rooibos
- Valerian Root & Chamomile Sleep Blend
- Cardamom & Ginger Chai
- Spearmint & Lemongrass Zest
- Green Tea & Jasmine Harmony
- Hawthorn Berry & Hibiscus Heart Tonic
- Moringa & Citrus Energizer
- Dandelion Root & Ginger Cleanse
- Apple & Cinnamon Cider Tea
- Chia Seed & Hibiscus Cooler
- Lemon Balm & Honey Calming Brew
- Ginseng & Green Tea Revitalizer
- Turmeric & Coconut Milk Latte
- Thyme & Rosemary Infusion

- Ginger & Lemongrass Revive
- Fennel Seed & Licorice Sweetness
- Juniper Berry & Mint Refresh
- Coconut & Vanilla Rooibos Delight
- Cinnamon & Ginger Hot Chocolate Infusion
- Saffron & Rose Petal Luxury Tea
- Orange Blossom & Chamomile Tranquility
- Elderberry & Ginger Winter Brew
- Mint & Lime Iced Infusion
- Pomegranate & Hibiscus Refresher
- Spicy Chai with Almond Milk
- Raspberry & Mint Sparkler
- Lemongrass & Ginger Chill
- Caramel & Hazelnut Herbal Brew

Chamomile & Lavender Dream Tea

Ingredients:

- 1 tablespoon dried chamomile flowers
- 1 teaspoon dried lavender buds
- 1 tablespoon honey (optional)
- 2 cups water
- Lemon slices (optional)

Instructions:

1. **Boil Water:** In a small saucepan, bring the water to a boil.
2. **Add Herbs:** Once boiling, remove the saucepan from heat and add the chamomile flowers and lavender buds.
3. **Steep:** Cover and let the herbs steep for about 5–10 minutes, depending on how strong you want the flavor.
4. **Strain:** After steeping, strain the tea into a cup to remove the flowers and buds.
5. **Sweeten (Optional):** Stir in honey if you like your tea sweet. You can also add a slice of lemon for extra flavor.
6. **Enjoy:** Sip your soothing tea in a quiet space to fully unwind.

Tips:

- You can also add a dash of vanilla extract for an extra layer of flavor.
- For a cold version, let the tea cool, then pour over ice and garnish with lemon.

Peppermint & Lemon Balm Refresh

Ingredients:

- 1 tablespoon dried peppermint leaves
- 1 tablespoon dried lemon balm leaves
- 2 cups water
- Honey or agave syrup (optional)
- Fresh lemon slices (optional)

Instructions:

1. **Boil Water:** Bring the water to a boil.
2. **Add Herbs:** Remove from heat and add the peppermint and lemon balm.
3. **Steep:** Cover and steep for 5–10 minutes.
4. **Strain:** Strain into a cup, sweeten if desired, and garnish with lemon slices.
5. **Enjoy:** Sip to refresh and rejuvenate!

Ginger & Turmeric Zing

Ingredients:

- 1-inch piece of fresh ginger, sliced
- 1-inch piece of fresh turmeric, sliced (or 1 teaspoon dried turmeric)
- 2 cups water
- Honey (optional)
- Lemon juice (optional)

Instructions:

1. **Boil Water:** Bring the water to a boil.
2. **Add Ginger and Turmeric:** Add the ginger and turmeric to the boiling water.
3. **Simmer:** Reduce heat and let simmer for 10 minutes.
4. **Strain:** Strain into a cup, sweeten with honey, and add lemon juice if desired.
5. **Enjoy:** Drink for a zesty and warming experience!

Hibiscus & Rose Hip Bliss

Ingredients:

- 1 tablespoon dried hibiscus flowers
- 1 tablespoon dried rose hips
- 2 cups water
- Honey or sugar (optional)
- Mint leaves for garnish (optional)

Instructions:

1. **Boil Water:** Bring the water to a boil.
2. **Add Herbs:** Remove from heat and add the hibiscus and rose hips.
3. **Steep:** Let steep for 10–15 minutes for a vibrant color and flavor.
4. **Strain:** Strain into a cup and sweeten if desired.
5. **Enjoy:** Garnish with mint leaves for a refreshing touch!

Lemon Verbena & Mint Cooler

Ingredients:

- 1 tablespoon dried lemon verbena leaves
- 1 tablespoon dried mint leaves
- 2 cups water
- Honey (optional)
- Lemon slices (optional)

Instructions:

1. **Boil Water:** Bring the water to a boil.
2. **Add Herbs:** Remove from heat and add lemon verbena and mint.
3. **Steep:** Cover and steep for 5–10 minutes.
4. **Strain:** Strain into a cup, sweeten if desired, and garnish with lemon slices.
5. **Enjoy:** Sip to refresh!

Sage & Honey Elixir

Ingredients:

- 1 tablespoon dried sage leaves
- 2 cups water
- Honey (to taste)
- Lemon juice (optional)

Instructions:

1. **Boil Water:** Bring the water to a boil.
2. **Add Sage:** Remove from heat and add sage leaves.
3. **Steep:** Let steep for 5–7 minutes.
4. **Strain:** Strain into a cup and stir in honey and lemon juice if desired.
5. **Enjoy:** A soothing and aromatic elixir!

Rooibos & Vanilla Comfort

Ingredients:

- 1 tablespoon rooibos tea
- 1 teaspoon vanilla extract (or 1 vanilla bean)
- 2 cups water
- Milk or cream (optional)
- Sweetener (optional)

Instructions:

1. **Boil Water:** Bring the water to a boil.
2. **Add Rooibos:** Remove from heat and add rooibos and vanilla.
3. **Steep:** Let steep for 5–7 minutes.
4. **Strain:** Strain into a cup, and add milk or sweetener if desired.
5. **Enjoy:** A comforting and creamy treat!

Elderflower & Lime Delight

Ingredients:

- 1 tablespoon dried elderflowers
- Juice of 1 lime
- 2 cups water
- Honey (optional)

Instructions:

1. **Boil Water:** Bring the water to a boil.
2. **Add Elderflowers:** Remove from heat and add elderflowers.
3. **Steep:** Let steep for 10 minutes.
4. **Strain:** Strain into a cup, stir in lime juice and honey if desired.
5. **Enjoy:** A refreshing and floral delight!

Nettle & Dandelion Detox

Ingredients:

- 1 tablespoon dried nettle leaves
- 1 tablespoon dried dandelion leaves
- 2 cups water
- Lemon juice (optional)

Instructions:

1. **Boil Water:** Bring the water to a boil.
2. **Add Herbs:** Remove from heat and add nettle and dandelion.
3. **Steep:** Let steep for 10 minutes.
4. **Strain:** Strain into a cup and add lemon juice if desired.
5. **Enjoy:** A cleansing herbal detox!

Cinnamon & Apple Spice

Ingredients:

- 1 cinnamon stick (or 1 teaspoon ground cinnamon)
- 1 apple, sliced
- 2 cups water
- Honey (optional)

Instructions:

1. **Boil Water:** Bring the water to a boil.
2. **Add Cinnamon and Apple:** Add the cinnamon and apple slices.
3. **Simmer:** Reduce heat and let simmer for 10 minutes.
4. **Strain:** Strain into a cup and sweeten if desired.
5. **Enjoy:** A warm and cozy drink!

Thyme & Lemon Throat Soother

Ingredients:

- 1 tablespoon fresh or dried thyme
- Juice of 1 lemon
- 2 cups water
- Honey (optional)

Instructions:

1. **Boil Water:** Bring the water to a boil.
2. **Add Thyme:** Remove from heat and add thyme.
3. **Steep:** Let steep for 5–10 minutes.
4. **Strain:** Strain into a cup and stir in lemon juice and honey if desired.
5. **Enjoy:** A soothing remedy for your throat!

Lemon Ginger & Cayenne Kick

Ingredients:

- 1-inch piece of fresh ginger, sliced
- Juice of 1 lemon
- 1/4 teaspoon cayenne pepper
- 2 cups water
- Honey (optional)

Instructions:

1. **Boil Water:** Bring the water to a boil.
2. **Add Ginger:** Remove from heat and add ginger.
3. **Simmer:** Let steep for 10 minutes.
4. **Strain:** Strain into a cup, stir in lemon juice, cayenne, and honey if desired.
5. **Enjoy:** A zesty and invigorating drink!

Holy Basil & Clove Calm

Ingredients:

- 1 tablespoon dried holy basil (tulsi)
- 2-3 whole cloves
- 2 cups water
- Honey (optional)

Instructions:

1. **Boil Water:** Bring the water to a boil.
2. **Add Herbs:** Remove from heat and add holy basil and cloves.
3. **Steep:** Let steep for 5–10 minutes.
4. **Strain:** Strain into a cup and sweeten if desired.
5. **Enjoy:** A calming and aromatic infusion!

Raspberry Leaf & Hibiscus Harmony

Ingredients:

- 1 tablespoon dried raspberry leaves
- 1 tablespoon dried hibiscus flowers
- 2 cups water
- Honey (optional)

Instructions:

1. **Boil Water:** Bring the water to a boil.
2. **Add Herbs:** Remove from heat and add raspberry leaves and hibiscus.
3. **Steep:** Cover and steep for 5–10 minutes.
4. **Strain:** Strain into a cup, sweeten if desired.
5. **Enjoy:** A refreshing and vibrant herbal tea!

Fennel & Anise Digestive Brew

Ingredients:

- 1 tablespoon fennel seeds
- 1 teaspoon anise seeds
- 2 cups water
- Honey (optional)

Instructions:

1. **Boil Water:** Bring the water to a boil.
2. **Add Seeds:** Remove from heat and add fennel and anise seeds.
3. **Steep:** Cover and steep for 5–7 minutes.
4. **Strain:** Strain into a cup and sweeten if desired.
5. **Enjoy:** A soothing brew for digestion!

Echinacea & Ginger Immune Booster

Ingredients:

- 1 tablespoon dried echinacea
- 1-inch piece of fresh ginger, sliced
- 2 cups water
- Honey (optional)
- Lemon juice (optional)

Instructions:

1. **Boil Water:** Bring the water to a boil.
2. **Add Herbs:** Remove from heat and add echinacea and ginger.
3. **Steep:** Let steep for 10 minutes.
4. **Strain:** Strain into a cup, add honey and lemon juice if desired.
5. **Enjoy:** A warming immune-boosting tea!

Licorice Root & Chamomile Serenity

Ingredients:

- 1 tablespoon dried licorice root
- 1 tablespoon dried chamomile flowers
- 2 cups water
- Honey (optional)

Instructions:

1. **Boil Water:** Bring the water to a boil.
2. **Add Herbs:** Remove from heat and add licorice root and chamomile.
3. **Steep:** Cover and steep for 5–10 minutes.
4. **Strain:** Strain into a cup, sweeten if desired.
5. **Enjoy:** A calming and soothing infusion!

Tulsi & Mint Refreshment

Ingredients:

- 1 tablespoon dried tulsi (holy basil)
- 1 tablespoon dried mint leaves
- 2 cups water
- Honey (optional)

Instructions:

1. **Boil Water:** Bring the water to a boil.
2. **Add Herbs:** Remove from heat and add tulsi and mint.
3. **Steep:** Cover and steep for 5–10 minutes.
4. **Strain:** Strain into a cup, sweeten if desired.
5. **Enjoy:** A refreshing and uplifting drink!

Orange Peel & Cardamom Cheer

Ingredients:

- 1 tablespoon dried orange peel
- 4-5 whole cardamom pods, crushed
- 2 cups water
- Honey (optional)

Instructions:

1. **Boil Water:** Bring the water to a boil.
2. **Add Ingredients:** Remove from heat and add orange peel and cardamom.
3. **Steep:** Cover and steep for 5–10 minutes.
4. **Strain:** Strain into a cup and sweeten if desired.
5. **Enjoy:** A fragrant and cheerful infusion!

Lavender & Lemonade Fusion

Ingredients:

- 1 tablespoon dried lavender buds
- Juice of 1 lemon
- 2 cups water
- Honey (optional)

Instructions:

1. **Boil Water:** Bring the water to a boil.
2. **Add Lavender:** Remove from heat and add lavender buds.
3. **Steep:** Let steep for 5–7 minutes.
4. **Strain:** Strain into a cup, add lemon juice and honey if desired.
5. **Enjoy:** A fragrant and refreshing drink!

Marshmallow Root & Peppermint Relief

Ingredients:

- 1 tablespoon dried marshmallow root
- 1 tablespoon dried peppermint leaves
- 2 cups water
- Honey (optional)

Instructions:

1. **Boil Water:** Bring the water to a boil.
2. **Add Herbs:** Remove from heat and add marshmallow root and peppermint.
3. **Steep:** Cover and steep for 10 minutes.
4. **Strain:** Strain into a cup, sweeten if desired.
5. **Enjoy:** A soothing and relieving herbal tea!

Yarrow & Ginger Immunity Boost

Ingredients:

- 1 tablespoon dried yarrow flowers
- 1-inch piece of fresh ginger, sliced
- 2 cups water
- Honey (optional)

Instructions:

1. **Boil Water:** Bring the water to a boil.
2. **Add Ingredients:** Remove from heat and add yarrow and ginger.
3. **Steep:** Let steep for 10 minutes.
4. **Strain:** Strain into a cup and sweeten if desired.
5. **Enjoy:** A warming and immune-boosting drink!

Chai Spiced Rooibos

Ingredients:

- 1 tablespoon rooibos tea
- 1/2 teaspoon cinnamon
- 1/4 teaspoon ginger (ground or fresh)
- 1/4 teaspoon cardamom (ground or crushed pods)
- 2 cups water
- Milk or cream (optional)
- Sweetener (optional)

Instructions:

1. **Boil Water:** Bring the water to a boil.
2. **Add Rooibos and Spices:** Remove from heat and add rooibos and spices.
3. **Steep:** Let steep for 5–7 minutes.
4. **Strain:** Strain into a cup and add milk and sweetener if desired.
5. **Enjoy:** A flavorful and cozy chai!

Valerian Root & Chamomile Sleep Blend

Ingredients:

- 1 tablespoon dried valerian root
- 1 tablespoon dried chamomile flowers
- 2 cups water
- Honey (optional)

Instructions:

1. **Boil Water:** Bring the water to a boil.
2. **Add Herbs:** Remove from heat and add valerian root and chamomile.
3. **Steep:** Cover and steep for 10 minutes.
4. **Strain:** Strain into a cup, sweeten if desired.
5. **Enjoy:** A calming blend to help you unwind!

Cardamom & Ginger Chai

Ingredients:

- 1 teaspoon black tea (or rooibos for caffeine-free)
- 1/2 teaspoon cardamom pods, crushed
- 1-inch piece of fresh ginger, sliced
- 2 cups water
- Milk or cream (optional)
- Sweetener (optional)

Instructions:

1. **Boil Water:** Bring the water to a boil.
2. **Add Ingredients:** Remove from heat and add tea, cardamom, and ginger.
3. **Steep:** Let steep for 5 minutes.
4. **Strain:** Strain into a cup and add milk and sweetener if desired.
5. **Enjoy:** A fragrant and spicy chai!

Spearmint & Lemongrass Zest

Ingredients:

- 1 tablespoon dried spearmint leaves
- 1 tablespoon dried lemongrass
- 2 cups water
- Honey (optional)

Instructions:

1. **Boil Water:** Bring the water to a boil.
2. **Add Herbs:** Remove from heat and add spearmint and lemongrass.
3. **Steep:** Cover and steep for 5–7 minutes.
4. **Strain:** Strain into a cup, sweeten if desired.
5. **Enjoy:** A refreshing and zesty infusion!

Green Tea & Jasmine Harmony

Ingredients:

- 1 tablespoon green tea leaves
- 1 tablespoon dried jasmine flowers
- 2 cups water

Instructions:

1. **Boil Water:** Bring the water to a boil, then let it cool slightly (about 175°F or 80°C).
2. **Add Ingredients:** Add green tea and jasmine to the water.
3. **Steep:** Let steep for 3–5 minutes.
4. **Strain:** Strain into a cup.
5. **Enjoy:** A fragrant and harmonious tea!

Hawthorn Berry & Hibiscus Heart Tonic

Ingredients:

- 1 tablespoon dried hawthorn berries
- 1 tablespoon dried hibiscus flowers
- 2 cups water
- Honey (optional)

Instructions:

1. **Boil Water:** Bring the water to a boil.
2. **Add Ingredients:** Remove from heat and add hawthorn and hibiscus.
3. **Steep:** Cover and steep for 10 minutes.
4. **Strain:** Strain into a cup, sweeten if desired.
5. **Enjoy:** A heart-healthy tonic!

Moringa & Citrus Energizer

Ingredients:

- 1 tablespoon dried moringa leaves
- Juice of 1 orange or lemon
- 2 cups water
- Honey (optional)

Instructions:

1. **Boil Water:** Bring the water to a boil.
2. **Add Moringa:** Remove from heat and add moringa leaves.
3. **Steep:** Let steep for 5–7 minutes.
4. **Strain:** Strain into a cup, add citrus juice and honey if desired.
5. **Enjoy:** A refreshing and energizing drink!

Dandelion Root & Ginger Cleanse

Ingredients:

- 1 tablespoon dried dandelion root
- 1-inch piece of fresh ginger, sliced
- 2 cups water
- Honey (optional)

Instructions:

1. **Boil Water:** Bring the water to a boil.
2. **Add Ingredients:** Remove from heat and add dandelion root and ginger.
3. **Steep:** Let steep for 10 minutes.
4. **Strain:** Strain into a cup, sweeten if desired.
5. **Enjoy:** A cleansing and detoxifying brew!

Apple & Cinnamon Cider Tea

Ingredients:

- 1 apple, sliced
- 1 cinnamon stick (or 1 teaspoon ground cinnamon)
- 2 cups water
- Honey (optional)
- Cloves (optional)

Instructions:

1. **Boil Water:** Bring the water to a boil.
2. **Add Apple and Cinnamon:** Add the apple slices and cinnamon stick.
3. **Simmer:** Reduce heat and let simmer for 10 minutes.
4. **Strain:** Strain into a cup and sweeten with honey if desired.
5. **Enjoy:** A warm and comforting tea!

Chia Seed & Hibiscus Cooler

Ingredients:

- 1 tablespoon dried hibiscus flowers
- 1 tablespoon chia seeds
- 2 cups water
- Honey or agave syrup (optional)
- Fresh lime juice (optional)

Instructions:

1. **Boil Water:** Bring the water to a boil.
2. **Add Hibiscus:** Remove from heat and add hibiscus flowers.
3. **Steep:** Let steep for 10 minutes.
4. **Strain:** Strain into a pitcher and stir in chia seeds.
5. **Chill:** Refrigerate until cool, then sweeten and add lime juice if desired.
6. **Enjoy:** A refreshing and hydrating drink!

Lemon Balm & Honey Calming Brew

Ingredients:

- 1 tablespoon dried lemon balm leaves
- 2 cups water
- Honey (to taste)

Instructions:

1. **Boil Water:** Bring the water to a boil.
2. **Add Lemon Balm:** Remove from heat and add lemon balm leaves.
3. **Steep:** Cover and steep for 5–10 minutes.
4. **Strain:** Strain into a cup and sweeten with honey.
5. **Enjoy:** A calming and soothing tea!

Ginseng & Green Tea Revitalizer

Ingredients:

- 1 teaspoon ginseng root (dried)
- 1 tablespoon green tea leaves
- 2 cups water
- Honey (optional)

Instructions:

1. **Boil Water:** Bring the water to a boil, then let cool slightly (about 175°F or 80°C).
2. **Add Ingredients:** Add ginseng and green tea to the water.
3. **Steep:** Let steep for 3–5 minutes.
4. **Strain:** Strain into a cup and sweeten if desired.
5. **Enjoy:** A revitalizing and energizing drink!

Turmeric & Coconut Milk Latte

Ingredients:

- 1 teaspoon ground turmeric (or 1-inch fresh turmeric, grated)
- 1 cup coconut milk
- 1 cup water
- Honey or maple syrup (optional)
- Cinnamon (optional)

Instructions:

1. **Boil Water:** Bring the water to a boil.
2. **Add Turmeric:** Remove from heat and whisk in turmeric.
3. **Heat Coconut Milk:** In a separate pan, heat coconut milk.
4. **Combine:** Mix the turmeric water and coconut milk together.
5. **Sweeten:** Stir in honey or syrup and sprinkle with cinnamon if desired.
6. **Enjoy:** A creamy and anti-inflammatory latte!

Thyme & Rosemary Infusion

Ingredients:

- 1 tablespoon dried thyme
- 1 tablespoon dried rosemary
- 2 cups water
- Lemon juice (optional)

Instructions:

1. **Boil Water:** Bring the water to a boil.
2. **Add Herbs:** Remove from heat and add thyme and rosemary.
3. **Steep:** Cover and steep for 5–10 minutes.
4. **Strain:** Strain into a cup and add lemon juice if desired.
5. **Enjoy:** A fragrant and herbal infusion!

Ginger & Lemongrass Revive

Ingredients:

- 1-inch piece of fresh ginger, sliced
- 1 stalk lemongrass, chopped
- 2 cups water
- Honey (optional)

Instructions:

1. **Boil Water:** Bring the water to a boil.
2. **Add Ginger and Lemongrass:** Remove from heat and add ginger and lemongrass.
3. **Steep:** Let steep for 10 minutes.
4. **Strain:** Strain into a cup and sweeten if desired.
5. **Enjoy:** A refreshing and revitalizing drink!

Fennel Seed & Licorice Sweetness

Ingredients:

- 1 tablespoon fennel seeds
- 1 teaspoon dried licorice root (or a small piece of fresh)
- 2 cups water
- Honey (optional)

Instructions:

1. **Boil Water:** Bring the water to a boil.
2. **Add Seeds and Licorice:** Remove from heat and add fennel seeds and licorice.
3. **Steep:** Cover and steep for 5–10 minutes.
4. **Strain:** Strain into a cup and sweeten with honey if desired.
5. **Enjoy:** A sweet and soothing herbal tea!

Juniper Berry & Mint Refresh

Ingredients:

- 1 tablespoon dried juniper berries
- 1 tablespoon dried mint leaves
- 2 cups water
- Honey (optional)

Instructions:

1. **Boil Water:** Bring the water to a boil.
2. **Add Ingredients:** Remove from heat and add juniper berries and mint.
3. **Steep:** Cover and steep for 5–10 minutes.
4. **Strain:** Strain into a cup and sweeten if desired.
5. **Enjoy:** A refreshing and aromatic drink!

Coconut & Vanilla Rooibos Delight

Ingredients:

- 1 tablespoon rooibos tea
- 1 tablespoon shredded coconut
- 1 teaspoon vanilla extract (or 1 vanilla bean)
- 2 cups water
- Milk or cream (optional)

Instructions:

1. **Boil Water:** Bring the water to a boil.
2. **Add Ingredients:** Remove from heat and add rooibos, coconut, and vanilla.
3. **Steep:** Let steep for 5–7 minutes.
4. **Strain:** Strain into a cup and add milk or cream if desired.
5. **Enjoy:** A creamy and delightful infusion!

Cinnamon & Ginger Hot Chocolate Infusion

Ingredients:

- 2 cups milk or a milk alternative
- 1 tablespoon cocoa powder
- 1/2 teaspoon ground cinnamon
- 1-inch piece of fresh ginger, sliced (or 1/2 teaspoon ground ginger)
- Sweetener (to taste)

Instructions:

1. **Heat Milk:** In a saucepan, gently heat the milk.
2. **Add Ingredients:** Stir in cocoa powder, cinnamon, and ginger.
3. **Simmer:** Let simmer for 5 minutes, stirring occasionally.
4. **Strain:** Strain into a cup and sweeten to taste.
5. **Enjoy:** A cozy and spiced hot chocolate!

Saffron & Rose Petal Luxury Tea

Ingredients:

- 1 teaspoon saffron threads
- 1 tablespoon dried rose petals
- 2 cups water
- Honey (optional)

Instructions:

1. **Boil Water:** Bring the water to a boil.
2. **Add Ingredients:** Remove from heat and add saffron and rose petals.
3. **Steep:** Cover and steep for 5–10 minutes.
4. **Strain:** Strain into a cup and sweeten if desired.
5. **Enjoy:** A luxurious and fragrant tea!

Orange Blossom & Chamomile Tranquility

Ingredients:

- 1 tablespoon dried chamomile flowers
- 1 teaspoon orange blossom water
- 2 cups water
- Honey (optional)

Instructions:

1. **Boil Water:** Bring the water to a boil.
2. **Add Chamomile:** Remove from heat and add chamomile flowers.
3. **Steep:** Let steep for 5–10 minutes.
4. **Strain:** Strain into a cup and stir in orange blossom water and honey if desired.
5. **Enjoy:** A calming and soothing tea!

Elderberry & Ginger Winter Brew

Ingredients:

- 1 tablespoon dried elderberries
- 1-inch piece of fresh ginger, sliced
- 2 cups water
- Honey (optional)

Instructions:

1. **Boil Water:** Bring the water to a boil.
2. **Add Ingredients:** Remove from heat and add elderberries and ginger.
3. **Steep:** Let steep for 10 minutes.
4. **Strain:** Strain into a cup and sweeten if desired.
5. **Enjoy:** A warming winter brew!

Mint & Lime Iced Infusion

Ingredients:

- 1 tablespoon dried mint leaves
- Juice of 1 lime
- 2 cups water
- Sweetener (optional)
- Lime slices (for garnish)

Instructions:

1. **Boil Water:** Bring the water to a boil.
2. **Add Mint:** Remove from heat and add mint leaves.
3. **Steep:** Let steep for 5–10 minutes.
4. **Strain:** Strain into a pitcher and cool in the fridge.
5. **Serve:** Add lime juice and sweeten if desired. Serve over ice with lime slices. Enjoy a refreshing iced infusion!

Pomegranate & Hibiscus Refresher

Ingredients:

- 1 tablespoon dried hibiscus flowers
- 1/4 cup pomegranate juice
- 2 cups water
- Sweetener (optional)

Instructions:

1. **Boil Water:** Bring the water to a boil.
2. **Add Hibiscus:** Remove from heat and add hibiscus flowers.
3. **Steep:** Cover and steep for 10 minutes.
4. **Strain:** Strain into a pitcher and stir in pomegranate juice. Sweeten if desired.
5. **Serve:** Chill in the fridge or serve over ice for a refreshing drink!

Spicy Chai with Almond Milk

Ingredients:

- 1 tablespoon black tea (or rooibos for caffeine-free)
- 1/2 teaspoon ground cinnamon
- 1/4 teaspoon ground ginger
- 1/4 teaspoon cardamom
- 2 cups water
- 1 cup almond milk
- Sweetener (to taste)

Instructions:

1. **Boil Water:** Bring the water to a boil.
2. **Add Spices and Tea:** Remove from heat and add the black tea, cinnamon, ginger, and cardamom.
3. **Steep:** Let steep for 5 minutes.
4. **Strain:** Strain into a saucepan and add almond milk.
5. **Heat:** Gently heat the mixture, sweetening to taste.
6. **Enjoy:** A warm and spicy chai treat!

Raspberry & Mint Sparkler

Ingredients:

- 1 cup fresh or frozen raspberries
- 1 tablespoon dried mint leaves (or a handful of fresh mint)
- 2 cups water
- Sparkling water
- Sweetener (to taste)
- Lime slices (for garnish)

Instructions:

1. **Boil Water:** Bring the water to a boil.
2. **Add Raspberries and Mint:** Remove from heat and add raspberries and mint.
3. **Steep:** Let steep for 10 minutes.
4. **Strain:** Strain into a pitcher and sweeten if desired.
5. **Serve:** Mix with sparkling water and garnish with lime slices. Enjoy a refreshing sparkler!

Lemongrass & Ginger Chill

Ingredients:

- 1 stalk lemongrass, chopped
- 1-inch piece of fresh ginger, sliced
- 2 cups water
- Sweetener (optional)
- Ice (for serving)

Instructions:

1. **Boil Water:** Bring the water to a boil.
2. **Add Lemongrass and Ginger:** Remove from heat and add lemongrass and ginger.
3. **Steep:** Let steep for 10 minutes.
4. **Strain:** Strain into a pitcher and sweeten if desired.
5. **Serve:** Chill in the fridge or serve over ice for a refreshing drink!

Caramel & Hazelnut Herbal Brew

Ingredients:

- 1 tablespoon roasted hazelnut tea (or herbal tea of your choice)
- 1 teaspoon caramel syrup (or to taste)
- 2 cups water
- Milk or cream (optional)

Instructions:

1. **Boil Water:** Bring the water to a boil.
2. **Add Tea:** Remove from heat and add hazelnut tea.
3. **Steep:** Let steep for 5–7 minutes.
4. **Strain:** Strain into a cup and stir in caramel syrup. Add milk or cream if desired.
5. **Enjoy:** A rich and nutty herbal brew!